Why Human

What makes us unique in the age of artificial intelligence

Epris E. Ezekiel

Copyright 2024© Epris E. Ezekiel

All rights reserved. This book is copyrighted and no part of it may be reproduced, distributed, or transmitted in any form or by any means, including photocopying, recording, or other electronic or mechanical methods, without the prior written permission of the publisher, except in the case of brief quotations embodied in critical reviews and certain other non-commercial uses permitted by copyright law.

**Printed in the United States of America
Copyright 2024© Epris E. Ezekiel**

Contents

Introduction 1

Chapter 1 3

Will AI become more humanlike in the future? 3

Chapter 2 10

In the AI Age, What Sets Humans Apart? 10

Chapter 3 19

Consequences for Work in the Future 19

Chapter 4 25

The Human Role in AI 25

Chapter 5 33

Can artificial intelligence develop intelligence? Similar to humans, conscious 33

and creative 33

Conclusion 44

Introduction

In today's fast-paced, technology-driven society, remarkable artificial intelligence and automation advances are present in our lives and work. Amid such rapid change, many people question their purpose and value in an increasingly digital society. However, the modern era has enabled humans to rediscover and cherish their uniqueness.

At first glance, computers and robots outperform humans in various areas, including processing speed and data analytics. However, diving more into the complicated tapestry of human experience, it becomes clear that we have qualities that technology cannot replace. Beyond logic and algorithms, humans possess emotional intelligence, heart intelligence, creativity, adaptability, and moral judgment, all of which are essential to our shared humanity.

Unfortunately, many people are ignorant of the distinct characteristics that distinguish them. The small nuances that make us genuinely human are occasionally neglected in a world frequently focused on productivity, efficiency, and visible accomplishments. Understanding and accepting our intrinsic talents enables us to find our position in an AI-powered future while enriching our lives and relationships with others. This article examines the distinctions between humans and computers, focusing on heart intelligence and the brain-heart relationship. By diving into humans' distinctive characteristics and the consequences for the future of work, we seek to shed light on the exceptional worth of human contributions in an increasingly digital world.

Chapter 1

Will AI become more humanlike in the future?

Similar to the space race of the 1950s, developers all around the world are striving to be the first to advance artificial intelligence. There are two approaches to making it more human: positive and negative.

In the worst-case scenario, AI would develop consciousness despite having no moral consciousness or emotional intelligence. An AI that lacks morality and consciousness is emotionally challenged. As shown in the so-called "paperclip dystopia," where AI makes limitless paperclips and learns to do it better and quicker, eventually turning people into them, such an AI may create countless or bothersome nuisances! Stephen Hawking reminded us that humans must be taken into consideration if AI becomes sentient.

Human experience should always be placed alongside or above artificial intelligence for precisely the reason described in the dystopia above. For the same reason, whenever I ask ChatGPT to perform something, I always say "please." Stated differently, in the best-case scenario, ethics and AI development are under human control. Communication and human control are the essential components. It is only at that point that consciousness, empathy, and awareness can arise.

In what way does AI affect humanity?

AIs are well-suited for any work requiring regular problem-solving inside preexisting structures, procedures, and knowledge bases. Indeed, there is already a growing automation in industries like customer service, travel planning, stock trading, real estate, and even apparel design. Researchers predict that, in contrast to previous waves of automation that primarily affected lower-wage, lower-educated workers, AI will also affect well-educated and well-paid "knowledge workers." Analysts and academics are closely monitoring how AI will affect the labor market of the future.

It was incorrect to believe that computers would take decades or perhaps centuries to catch up to the agile human intellect, even though we're nonetheless a long way from computers that can function flawlessly as individuals. Deep learning's exponential growth is enabling AI to converse with humans in a nearly human manner, identify diseases more accurately than a physician, and possibly even deceive us shortly. For the most part, humanity has been forced to dedicate its existence to ensuring its survival, except for a very small number of people. Higher-level pursuits like scientific research, art, music, and philosophy are beyond the reach of most people's time or energy. However, those activities should be considered requirements rather than frills as the human race confronts the threat of potential obsolescence. We have an unprecedented and urgent opportunity to identify the distinctive value humanity delivers and to foster the uniquely human abilities that produce that value, even as technology eats away at the repetitive jobs that most people have historically done to make a living.

Developing the human advantage

Humans are a species that is motivated to try new things, push limits, create something valuable, and change the world. Humans have strong inclinations to explore, enjoy novelty, and take risks. However, if we don't nurture these impulses, they will eventually fade.

Artificial intelligence is excellent at producing fresh insights from current data and automating repetitive knowledge tasks. It is unable to infer the presence of information that it is not currently aware of, let alone the potential of it. Radical new business models are beyond its imagination. Might pose inquiries that weren't previously thought out. Or picture unthinkable chances and triumphs.

It lacks basic sense entirely! The fact that ropes can pull but not push, or that water is moist, is unknown to robots (until you tell it). Furthermore, "intellectual capitalism" activities involving innovation, imagination, leadership, analysis, comedy, and creative ideas are not something that robots can perform.

However, we have only just started to give these so-called "soft skills" more weight in our educational systems. Most of the time, we still assume that people will develop their emotional intelligence, cross-cultural awareness, curiosity, critical thinking, and tenacity naturally—as if these are just traits that come with time. But these abilities are not delicate in the slightest. They are essential, pedagogically teachable, and a crucial distinction between artificial and human intelligence.

Human Touch

While AI can handle a wide range of activities, human talents such as emotional intelligence, creativity, and strategic thinking remain very significant. These skills allow people to supplement AI technologies, resulting in more original and successful solutions.

Prepare for the Future

Workers, employers, and policymakers must work together to maximize the benefits of AI and effectively manage its challenges as it evolves. This includes investing in education and training, fostering a culture of lifelong learning, and developing policies that help workers transition into new roles created by AI.

Ethical AI

Workers will play a critical role in ensuring AI systems are created and implemented ethically, according to ethical norms, and minimizing bias. As AI becomes more integrated into the tech industry, the necessity of ethical considerations grows.

Chapter 2

In the AI Age, What Sets Humans Apart?

It's natural to question, as AI permeates more and more aspects of our daily lives, what distinguishes humans in this era of sentient machines.

I just heard someone state that "humans are just a bunch of code, and AI is the future."

What distinguishes humans from AI in a world where machines are developing at a breakneck pace? What makes us more than a jumble of numbers and formulas?

The Influence of Social Attachment

In a technologically driven world, it is simple to overlook the importance of human connection, but here is another area in which humans excel over AI: we can create meaningful, long-lasting relationships with others. Whether they are romantic, platonic, or familial, these bonds are based on mutual respect, trust, and shared experiences.

Artificial intelligence (AI) may be able to simulate a conversation or provide information, but it will never be able to fully replace the moments that bring joy and fulfillment to life, like sitting down with a friend and laughing over a cup of coffee or feeling warmly hugged or comforted by someone who means genuinely caring about you.

The Human Touch: Sentiment and Compassion

Our feelings are the first thing that springs to mind. We can experience a vast spectrum of emotions, including happiness, sadness, rage, love, and everything in between, unlike robots. We can interact with people on a level that AI just cannot match because of this emotional depth. We are capable of far more than any machine whether we laugh together, cry together, or lend a consoling hand.

Another important thing that sets humans apart from AI is empathy. While AI may be able to analyze data and predict behavior, it is unable to truly comprehend what it means to be human, which includes being able to sympathize with us in our moments of need or truly offering comfort when things are tough. Only another human can do these things.

Flaws: The Allure of Having Defects

The other thing that sets humans apart is our flaws. While AI aims for accuracy and flawlessness, humans are inherently flawed, and that's a good thing. Most mistakes teach us valuable lessons that help us grow as people and become resilient, creative, and more aware of the world. Imperfections: The Beauty of Being Flawed

Yet in their pursuit of perfection, machines cannot experience the growth that comes from making mistakes; our imperfections, and the lessons we learn from them, are an essential component of what makes us human. In contrast, machines are built to minimize errors. They function on the principle of efficiency, carrying out tasks with accuracy that we can't always match.

What Sets Humans Apart from Ai

Human value is increasingly being evaluated in robotics, AI, and machine learning skills. But this viewpoint falls short of defining what it is to be human. Our distinctiveness is found in the intangible qualities that characterize who we are as people, not in the speed at which our brains process information or in our capacity for repetitive action. What makes us genuinely different from others is how we think, feel, and interact. It's more crucial than ever to embrace our human traits and realize their significance at a time when machines seem to be invading every part of our lives.

A concept that most people are unaware of is the interaction between the heart and brain, known as heart intelligence. But it is important to take into account because it emphasizes even more the fundamental distinctions between computers and people.

morality and ethics
When deciding on an ethical course of action, humans are capable of considering various viewpoints, values, and outcomes. Although they are capable of adhering to moral standards, computers are not sensitive to the subtle

differences in morality.

After taking the aforementioned into account, we can conclude that the qualities that make us human are more defining than our brain's processing speed or our capacity for repeated work. True uniqueness comes from our thoughts, emotions, and interpersonal relationships. Appreciating our human traits and realizing their value is crucial now more than ever in a time when technology seems to be invading every part of our lives.

Being Flexible and Adaptable

Without set guidelines, humans can adapt and learn in different environments. Computers are less adaptable in fresh settings since they depend on algorithms and data.

Comprehensive Knowledge

For a comprehensive understanding, humans can combine many knowledge sources, take context into account, and draw from personal experiences. Computers handle data in a more data-driven and segmented manner.

Being self-aware and Conscious
People can reflect on their thoughts, feelings, and experiences by going inward and using their consciousness and self-awareness. Encouraging oneself and making moral decisions are aided by this self-awareness. In contrast, computers are neither conscious nor aware of themselves.

Innovation and Creativity
Intuition, imagination, and creative problem-solving are all components of human creativity. Although computers may produce novel outputs based on data and patterns, they are not capable of the impulsive creativity and intuitive leaps

that characterize human innovation.

Sensations and Compassion

Because of our emotional intelligence, humans can recognize, feel, and react to a variety of emotions. This capacity promotes compassion, empathy, and complex social connections. Though they can't feel emotions, computers can mimic emotional reactions.

The Link Between the Brain and Heart

There is a strong correlation between the heart and the brain in humans that is frequently disregarded in the discussion of AI. In addition to being physiological, this brain-heart interaction is both intuitive and affective. The heart has a sophisticated neural system and is an organ in addition to being a mechanical pump. There are neurological, pharmacological, biophysical, and energetic pathways via which this "heart-brain" in our brains can exchange information with the central brain. Within the human body, these channels function in tandem to form an intricate and comprehensive communication system.

In contrast to what the brain sends to the heart, the heart transmits more information to the brain. Perception, emotional processing, and higher-order cognitive processes can all be modulated by this knowledge. It may also be detected several feet from the body, the electromagnetic field of the heart being roughly 60 times stronger than the electrical activity coming from the brain. Every cell in our body is a part of this field, which extends into the surrounding area in every direction. Using instruments like heart rate variability (HRV) analysis, one may measure how the heart's field changes noticeably as we feel different emotions.

Chapter 3

Consequences for Work in the Future

Positions Suitable for Substitution

Automating routine, rule-based tasks that demand minimal emotional intelligence or human judgment is a great idea. Tasks involving pattern recognition, such as fraud detection and picture analysis, can also be automated.

Careers in Which Human Skills Are Essential

Emotionally intelligent, creative, complicated problem-solving and morally judgment-based jobs are less interchangeable. These encompass social work, healthcare, education, the arts, and positions of leadership.

Knowledge for the Digital Age

The abilities that set humans apart from machines should be prioritized by humans:

- ❖ **Ethical Assessment:** It's important to

weigh the implications, values, and views of various parties while making decisions.

- ❖ **Flexible:** These are essential skills: learning, developing, and adapting to new environments and technology.
- ❖ **The relationship between emotional and heart intelligence:** Effective communication, empathy, and compassion are made possible by developing one's heart and emotional intelligence.
- ❖ **Imagination and Analysis:** What makes humans unique is our ability to think creatively, invent, and solve challenging issues.

Humans should emphasize the distinctive traits that distinguish people from machines as AI changes the workplace. Humans may prosper in an AI-driven society by embracing heart intelligence, emotional intelligence, creativity, adaptability, and ethical judgment, and by using technology to augment rather than replace their innate skills.

Artificial Intelligence and Human Intelligence Coexisting

The future holds the cohabitation of human intellect and artificial intelligence (AI) systems as AI develops and becomes more and more integrated into our daily lives. This synergy has a lot of potential for reciprocal improvement and complementary strengths that can help a lot of different areas of society. Future interactions, employment, and lifestyle will be influenced by the coexistence of AI and human intellect.

The following areas will be the main places where cohabitation occurs:

Moral as well as Ethical Aspects

The coexistence of AI with human intelligence

presents moral and ethical issues, even though AI has many advantages. Privacy, data security, and decision autonomy become more pressing issues as AI systems advance in sophistication. It's critical to establish rules and laws that protect human agency and control while guaranteeing the moral and responsible application of AI.

Innovations in Healthcare

With AI's ability to help with diagnosis, treatment planning, and monitoring, healthcare could undergo a revolutionary change. AI may examine medical data to identify early disease indicators and forecast patient outcomes, including test findings and imaging data. Human healthcare providers can use these insights to develop individualized treatments, make better decisions, and act quickly.

Customized Education and Development
By customizing educational materials and content to meet each student's requirements and interests, AI-driven systems may personalize learning experiences. AI can assist with knowledge gap identification, recommend pertinent readings, and modify training speed. Teachers may deliver more efficient and individualized student support through AI, encouraging lifelong learning and personal development.

Developing Creativity in Humans
The use of AI to enhance human creativity has shown promise. Through suggestion-making, work automation, and the creation of new art forms, AI-powered tools can support designers, artists, and other creatives. These tools allow people to focus on higher-level creative activities, such as pushing the envelope and

discovering new artistic expressions, with more time and energy available to them.

Working Together to Make Decisions

With the use of deep data analysis and machine learning, artificial intelligence (AI) systems can quickly process large volumes of data, identify patterns, and make predictions. However, humans also bring with them emotional intelligence, intuition, morality, and a comprehensive comprehension of intricate circumstances. Artificial intelligence and human decision-making can work together to produce more informed and well-rounded conclusions by combining data-driven insights and ethical concerns.

Chapter 4

The Human Role in AI

The integration of AI tools and technologies into a modern business necessitates a clear understanding of the role AI technology plays in the roles that only people can complete. Although some pundits predict that AI will eventually replace human labor in all tasks, the situation is not nearly that dire.

In areas where speed and efficiency are critical, artificial intelligence (AI) is displacing humans. It can work faster than a human and doesn't get tired because, well, it's a machine. For this reason, we're seeing AI take over simple, repetitive tasks that take a lot of human time. One such example is entity resolution.

Entity resolution refers to the method by which companies combine and align data from several silos and systems to produce a "golden record" that perfectly captures an important business entity, such as a patient, supplier, customer, or product. A person, a group of people, or even traditional technologies like rules-based master data management (MDM) would need an excessive amount of time to resolve entities throughout an organization's constantly expanding and changing data collection. The process would also restart any time new data entered the computers or when the data changed.

Entity resolution, however, becomes tenfold more effective when AI is used. Organizations can use AI to produce golden records, or the best possible representation of the data, fast and easily by utilizing sophisticated AI and machine learning-driven matching models. Nor do the models require rewriting or redefinition of the rules in response to data changes or new data brought to the system. Thus, rather than months or years, businesses see returns in a matter of weeks.

The heavy lifting involved in comparing and resolving data sets is assumed by AI in this instance. It is possible to promptly incorporate newly acquired data into the system and resolve it against already-existing entities, whether it comes from natural sources or through data enrichment. It optimizes a repetitious, time-consuming job by replacing a human or antiquated technology in the best way feasible. However, AI by itself is insufficient because it relies solely on the data used to train it.

Although AI is capable of matching and resolving entities based on the knowledge it has gained from the training data, humans are still needed to correct mistakes, render decisions in unclear situations, or provide further context that the AI might not have thought of. To guarantee the greatest degree of precision and dependability in both the AI models and the golden records it generates, human involvement in the process is essential.

When AI is used in conjunction with humans, the former spends more time providing value, context, and perspective through feedback and less time on the repetitive, boring duties connected with entity resolution. This enhances the reliability and integrity of the golden records. The efficiency and scalability of AI combined with human knowledge, feeling, and empathy are the best of both worlds when combined with human refinement.

The Significance of Human-AI Collaboration

Human supervision and cooperation are crucial,

even when artificial intelligence has the potential to change the industry. The application of empathy, creativity, and contextual relevance is where humans excel, while AI's strengths are in processing speeds and sophisticated algorithms.

Businesses must place a high priority on accepting responsibility for moral decision-making and the appropriate application of AI. They need to consider if they are adopting and using AI properly and if they are doing the correct things. An excellent starting point would be to encourage human-AI collaboration.

Including people in the process can assist in reinforcing the integrity of the AI and hold companies responsible for using it ethically by exposing potential biases, providing context, and introducing new concerns. Organizations face the danger of making bad judgments or damaging their reputations without this human refinement.

The following are the risks that firms run when they don't integrate human monitoring into their AI process.

Disregarding the context's importance
When AI is used without context, it may misunderstand data and produce biased, erroneous, or invalid results. Because of this, people need to take responsibility and improve the outcomes by providing context based on their past experiences. Without this important knowledge, data may be interpreted incorrectly and distorted, which could result in poor choices or undesirable results. However, when people are involved, they may assess and improve the AI by using their judgment and domain knowledge to make decisions in unclear circumstances or by

adding pertinent context that the AI would not have thought about.

The improvement of AI-driven outcomes depends heavily on humans. Without their input, AI may fail to consider important scenarios, ignore vital context, or, worse, reveal prejudice. Organizations may, however, improve the integrity of the results and achieve better commercial outcomes when people and AI work together.

Revealing Possible Bias

AI runs on data. Furthermore, poor data also produces poor AI outcomes. Nevertheless, inaccurate data might also have unintended effects. Users may be misled into believing anything or coming to a biased choice when the training data is skewed, inaccurate, outdated, or incomplete. When findings seem skewed or inaccurate, humans can help lower the likelihood of bias by correcting the models and providing context and insight that the AI might not have thought of.

Disregarding novel possibilities

Because of their individual experiences, humans possess a special capacity for imagining and creating new scenarios. The scenarios that people imagine are also unique because people have diverse experiences and makeup. Contrarily, AI is still unable to think through possibilities and circumstances outside of those it has been trained. Consequently, it can unintentionally overlook novel or distinct scenarios that exist outside the purview of its training data, or it might overlook possible use cases that only a person could imagine.

Chapter 5

Can artificial intelligence develop intelligence? Similar to humans, conscious and creative

Sensible behavior as opposed to intelligence

It is assumed that we are familiar with the definition of "intelligence" when we discuss artificial intelligence. There isn't a definition of intelligence that is accepted by everyone, though. Maybe artificial intelligence belongs in a different category and is not intended to be a direct replica of human intelligence.

Take the term "intelligence" as an example. Its meaning is "to comprehend," and it comes from the Latin word "intellect." Thus, to be intelligent is to understand intelligence and its possible ramifications (the "why") in addition to being able to mimic intelligence.

Using an autonomous vehicle as an example, how intelligent do you think it is? When someone crosses the street, does a car "understand" why it should stop? Does it share our human awareness of the surroundings? The fact that the car doesn't stop is evident, of course.

Realizes that it would injure the person or is acting in an attempt to prevent harm to the person. Not because of any inference of free will, but rather because it has been educated that way using the available evidence.

Despite appearances, feeding machine data and providing it with an algorithm is reproduction rather than intelligence. Some may say that people only follow regulations, but in most cases, this comes after careful consideration. We consider the intent of the rules, i.e., we assess whether they make sense to us given our knowledge. Therefore, we may say that a self-driving car that uses narrow artificial intelligence is not clever; rather, it is behaving intelligently.

Can human intellect and artificial intelligence be comparable or identical? We're not there yet with narrow AI if intelligence is associated with "understanding." We must address this matter, though, when it comes to artificial general intelligence.

What, though, is a reliable indicator of human intelligence? Alan Turing developed the now-famous Turing test in 1950 to explore this subject and determine whether a machine could mimic human intellect. The exam functions as follows and was once known as the "Imitation Game."

Envision a scenario in which two participants are humans and one is a machine, and all three are separated from one another. Like you might have with your buddies on your computer or smartphone, all of their interactions are text-based. The machine and the other person are being questioned by one person who is acting in the role of an interrogator. Both make an effort to respond to those inquiries to show the interrogator that they are human. If the test-taker is unable to determine which one is a human, the machine passes.

When a machine can fool a human into thinking it is a human instead of a machine, it has proven to have intelligent behavior, according to the test's ultimate result. Does a machine that passes this test, however, necessarily exhibit intellect comparable to that of a human if an observer is unable to distinguish between a machine and a human in this situation? Beyond intelligence, surely, there must be more to being human.

Originality

Since the dawn of time, one of the most distinctive qualities of humans has been our capacity for creativity. Considering whether or not a computer is capable of creativity is important if our goal is to create machines increasingly more like humans. The article AI and Visual Arts delves deeper into the ways that AI may support and foster our creativity.

In many cases, algorithms can conclude data in ways that humans could never. Within minutes, they can produce original music tailored to the needs of the client and paint like the well-known Edmond de Belamy image 4. Ray Kurzweil gave a 1965 demonstration of one of the earliest computer-generated music pieces that can be regarded as the forerunner of AI-generated compositions5. Thereafter, this field saw several applications.

As long as the correct input data is available,

machines are highly specialized and capable of producing nearly any kind of output. Can we classify this as creative work, even if it's remarkable and appears to be one? Is it solely because of the machine's ability to process pre-existing data? Could a machine make something fresh from nothing too? The majority of these artificially produced objects still seem a little strange, a little awkward, and a little non-human at this point. But after AI systems fix these errors, what will happen?

It's possible that an AI application won't need to be creative because we won't be aiming for a human-like AI. Could an AI system that lacks creativity be just as strong as one that does? The famous quote from Einstein reads, "Knowledge is limited, therefore imagination is more important." The capacity to use imagination to create anything is known as creativity, and the first step in this process is to be inquisitive and ask questions.

Would a computer that was fed all the knowledge available on logic, physics, and mathematics be able to develop the theory of relativity? Would an intelligent machine ask the "right" questions out of curiosity? Though we may never be able to fully imagine a machine doing this, perhaps our imagination is restricted.

A state of consciousness

We believe that consciousness is a trait shared by all people. Conscientia is a Latin word that means "knowing" in the sense of "being aware," and it is the source of the English word consciousness.

Depending on the situation, the phrase can have a variety of meanings. It is possible that we will want to distinguish between ideas of consciousness that range from animals to humans ("I think therefore I am"), or we may want to distinguish between distinct states or levels of consciousness, such as sleep, dreaming, and meditation. We consider three intuitive concepts that are widely accepted: subjectivity, awareness, and the capacity for experiencing or feeling. The concept of "consciousness" is difficult to define or comprehend altogether.

Research appears to support the idea that a particular level of intelligence may be necessary for the development of awareness. The degree to which certain animals exhibit (self-)consciousness[2] is nearly identical to that of humans, including dolphins and grey parrots. Elevated IQs seem to provide greater opportunities for awareness.

But may we also conclude that something can have or develop awareness if it is (or acts) intelligently? If we were to infer that a machine that passes the Turing test is human-like, the answer would most likely be "yes." The capacities for experiencing and feeling, however, which we frequently identify with consciousness, are not included in this.

The majority of philosophers believe that the subjective experience is what makes consciousness what it is. When you move and engage with others, when you smell something, and when you are hot or cold, you experience some sort of inner feeling. It appears that developing and having consciousness depend heavily on your capacity to sense and experience your surroundings.

When using AI, these observations bring up the

following three philosophical issues:

- ✓ What are the consequences if that's the case?
- ✓ Developing awareness in a machine?
- ✓ Is it possible to build a (aware) machine?

It is difficult to determine whether a machine can develop consciousness since we still do not fully understand what consciousness is or what is required for it to develop. To put it another way, there's a chance that we will create an AI with a purpose unrelated to the development of consciousness, yet it will still evolve.

How will we be able to tell when AI has become sentient? Think about a clever artificial intelligence system that uses a variety of sensors to monitor its surroundings. The question of whether consciousness is a simulation or a real thing arises even in the case of the prerequisites—intellect, and feeling, for example—that we believe are important for its development. Or put another way, how is our brain not only simulating the real environment around us? Let's assume we can develop an artificial intelligence system that can accurately represent its surroundings to further investigate these issues. It has the same ability to detect temperature, much like human skin. But could it also "feel" this? And would an AI even understand what it meant if it could read your face and decide whether you seem happy or sad? Does it make sense? What about experiences that are incomparable to us as humans? When AI is in flight mode, energy-saving mode, or runs out of RAM or hard drive space, does it sense anything?

Conclusion

As the AI era gets underway, people need to remember what makes them different from machines—their special qualities and skills. What AI cannot imitate are the intricate relationships between our hearts and brains, the dynamic nature of our emotional intelligence, and the adaptability of human intuition. Artificial intelligence, no matter how sophisticated or clever, will never be able to match human heart intelligence—a special combination of mental and emotional abilities. This is the primary factor that sets humans apart from machines.

Emotional intelligence coexists with rationality in human nature. Our emotional connection, empathy, love, and feelings are profound. Emotions and feelings have a role in the decisions we make in addition to reason and reasoning. We call this kind of intelligence "heart intelligence," since it allows us to make judgments based on both reason and feeling. AI can't compete in this field.

www.ingramcontent.com/pod-product-compliance
Lightning Source LLC
Chambersburg PA
CBHW070948220526
45471CB00007B/2938